5 REASONS
TO BELIEVE
IN RECENT CREATION

HENRY M. MORRIS III

INSTITUTE
for CREATION
RESEARCH

Dallas, Texas
www.icr.org

5 Reasons to Believe in Recent Creation

by Henry M. Morris III, D.Min.

First printing: November 2008
Fifth printing: February 2011

ISBN-13: 978-0-932766-91-5
ISBN-10: 0-932766-91-9

Please visit our website for other books and resources: www.icr.org.

Printed in the United States of America.

Cover image credit: NASA Johnson Space Center, www.nasa.gov.

CONTENTS

INTRODUCTION

One of the more annoying dilemmas among evangelicals today is the effort on the part of a growing number of technically and theologically trained Christians to wed the evolutionary doctrine of naturalistic development with the biblical account of creation that is recorded in the book of Genesis. Various hybrid theories have waxed and waned over the past 150 years, but all of them have unfortunately emanated from Christians, not from evolutionists. Naturalistic and atheistic evolutionists are content to ignore and exclude every religious text, especially the Bible.

Although some Christians believe it is possible to pick and choose the parts of the Bible they would like to follow and either ignore or deny the rest, that self-pleasing censorship is certainly not consistent with the message of the Bible. "Every word of God is pure," the Scripture insists. "Add thou not unto his words, lest he reprove thee, and thou be found a liar" (Proverbs 30:5-6).

So why is there confusion surrounding the account of creation in Genesis 1 and 2? Is there any merit to the so-called scientific claims of millions and billions of years of biological development? Is Scripture ambiguous on the issues related to the origin of life, the entrance of death, or the awful flood of Noah's day? Was the Genesis record simply written as a symbolic framework for later generations to adapt as needed in light of scientific discoveries?

The evidence—both biblical and scientific—suggests otherwise.

This book will examine the five most obvious reasons that an evolutionary worldview is both unbiblical and unscientific. A right understanding of the biblical account of creation is especially important for those who trust their eternal destiny to Jesus Christ, the One who proclaims Himself to be the Creator of everything that exists. Common sense would dictate that God's revealed Word must be true—or the God of the Bible is a fraud and a liar.

Reason 1

The Bible Does Not Allow an Evolutionary Interpretation

The biblical account of creation is not restricted only to the book of Genesis. References to creation are made throughout the Bible except in the one-chapter personal epistles of Paul, John, and Jude (Philemon; 2 and 3 John; Jude). Many of the great promises of God are based on the evidence of His creative power and work. The creation is not merely an allegorical story intended for moral instruction; it is treated throughout the rest of the Bible as a historical occurrence and is specifically documented as such.

The New Testament gospels record that the Lord Jesus alluded to the early chapters of Genesis no fewer than 25 times, with some additional 175 references cited or referred to by the writers of the New Testament. In each instance, the incident is cited as real history rather than allegory or metaphor from which we might simply derive a "spiritual" meaning. Either Jesus was speaking truth (as "the way, the truth, and the life," John 14:6), or He was Himself deluded, or worse, lying to accommodate the supposed "scientific ignorance" of the day.

The Bible Has No Hint of Evolutionary Development

Ultimately, since no human was around to observe the origin of the universe, we must all begin with presuppositional belief. Either God's Word is true about the creation, or modern scientific "theory" is true about the ages-long evolutionary development of all things through random processes. They cannot both be true. They are mutually exclusive.

Let there be no doubt. The Bible contains no reference, no inference, no metaphorical allegory—indeed, no hint of evolutionary development from simple to more complex life forms by blind, random chance. Nature, Psalm 19 boldly insists, has "speech" and "knowledge" that every day and every night declare the glory of God. "The creation," Paul affirms in Romans 1:20, manifests even the "invisible things" of God so that they are "clearly seen" in the physical and visible universe that He has created. Design, order, purpose, promises, goals, prophecy—all are "written" into the worlds that God has made. Nowhere does Scripture give credence to an evolutionary theory of origins.

Genesis 1:1 through 2:4 details the creation account carefully and thoroughly, day by day. So precise is the language that it appears that God carefully chose both the terms and the grammar to ensure that we could not mistake their meanings. God even makes a distinction between "creating" (bringing something into existence where nothing existed before), and "making" and "shaping" that which was created. God "spoke" and it was done (Psalm 33:9). God "commanded" and the great host of heaven was created (Psalm 148:5).

Any time man attempts to discover *how* God created, using his natural mind and his present ability to test and verify the processes of nature, he is doomed to failure. The Bible declares that "the worlds were framed by the word of God, so that things which are seen were not made of things which do appear" (Hebrews 11:3). The "science" of man is limited to merely what can be observed, as well as by a finite intellect with which man reasons, attempts to theorize, devises various tests, and tries to describe omnipotence!

Evolution is a story invented by man in order to exclude God from his life. Others have adapted it and tried to force an interpretation of Genesis in which God allegedly uses mechanistic and naturalistic processes to "create." Modern man is really good at telling the story of evolution! But that is *not* what the Bible says or teaches. Not even close.

The gospel of John begins by specifically identifying Jesus Christ as the Creator of all things (John 1:1-3). Paul confirms this in greater detail in Colossians 1:15-16:

> Who is the image of the invisible God, the firstborn of every creature: For by him were all things created, that are in heaven, and that are in earth, visible and invisible, whether they be thrones, or dominions, or principalities, or powers: all things were created by him, and for him.

Christ alone—not natural laws or evolutionary processes—is worthy "to receive glory and honour and power," because it is Christ alone who created all things (Revelation 4:11). His careful omniscient and omnipotent work could never be attributed to evolutionary processes and still conform to the truth given in the biblical record.

The simple fact is that God had no need to use evolutionary "ages" in His creation. The omnipotent and omniscient power of the Creator is the basis for all our trust in God. To anyone who reads the obvious attributes of God identified in the pages of Scripture, it is undeniable that God has the capability of creating the universe in six days. There is no reason to diminish the work of God by attributing it to time and chance; and less reason to doubt His written words. The creation did not take billions of years by means of natural processes; it took merely a word and all was accomplished, to last in its wholeness forever (Psalm 148:3-6).

Faith, which all thinking beings must have to exist in our universe, can either be foolish (e.g., the moon is made out of green cheese) or, as the Bible defines it, "the substance of things hoped for, the evidence of things not seen" (Hebrews 11:1). Science places an enormous amount of faith in the promise that God Himself made in Genesis 8:22:

> While the earth remaineth, seedtime and harvest, and cold
> and heat, and summer and winter, and day and night shall
> not cease.

Science, even evolutionary science, bases its theories, its predictions, and its conclusions on the stability of physical laws. Evolutionary science makes the mistake of extending the promise of God for stability in *this* world backwards to the processes of creation at the beginning of the world.

Living faith in God begins with faith in His work as Creator (Hebrews 11:3). What exists in the world today was not crafted or developed from pre-existing material. It was made specifically and instantaneously from nothing by the omnipotent and omniscient special creation of God.

The Bible's Language Is Precise about the Duration of Creation

The very concept of our "day" is defined explicitly in the first chapter of Genesis. "And God called the light Day, and the darkness he called Night. And the evening and the morning were the first day" (Genesis 1:5).

Just as time is measured in the present by days that are defined by the passage of the sun, so time began to be measured by God as the darkness (night = evening) passed into light (day = morning). That first cycle, the night-day cycle, was called Day One. The same formula is repeated for each of the six working days of God's initial work week. Once again, God seems to go out of His way to make sure that we could not mistake what He meant. Surely there is no more clear way to define the time involved than the specific word choices of Genesis 1.

Later, with His own finger, God wrote on the stone tablets of the Ten Commandments: "Six days shalt thou labor, and do all thy work: but the seventh day is the sabbath of the Lord...for in six days the Lord made heaven and earth, the sea, and all that in them is, and rested on the seventh day" (Exodus 20:9-11). This comparison between the six days of labor that all men experience and the seven days of the creation cannot possibly be taken as an allegorical allusion to immeasurable eons.

The only stated reason in Scripture why God did not create the entire universe in a single day is that God intended the creation week to be a template so man would know how to best function with the life God had created. God, who needs no rest for Himself, in His compassion anticipated and planned for man's rest. Jesus gave the reason: "The Sabbath was made for man, and not man for the sabbath" (Mark 2:27).

This "regular" day that God established in the creation week is denoted in Hebrew by the word *yowm* (plural *yamim*). That word is used over 3,000 times in the Old Testament. In Genesis 1:5, it is precisely delineated as the passing of darkness into light, or one solar day. It is coupled with the expression "evening and morning" 38 times, and is accompanied by a numerical modifier 359 times (e.g., eighth day, seventeenth day, etc.). The plural form appears 845 times. In none of the above 1,242 references can the word mean anything other than a literal, 24-hour, solar day. The context is absolutely clear.

The rest of the 1,758 times the Hebrew word *yowm* appears in its singular form are *never* used to speak of an eon-long age. Occasionally, "day" may be used to identify an unspecified period of time, as in the "day of trouble" (Psalm 20:1) or the "day of the Lord" (used 24 times in the Old Testament) or, as is in the case of Genesis 2:4, "in the day that the Lord God made the earth and the heavens." The only reason to translate "day" as "age" is to accommodate the required eons of evolution. Evolutionary thinking must have long, inexplicable, unthinkable ages to work and cannot accept the literal six-day creation that is recorded in Genesis.

The First Verse Is God's First Test of Faith

In the beginning God created the heaven and the earth. (Genesis 1:1)

Some have suggested that God set down a "faith test" with this very first of His words to His creation. Obviously, Genesis 1:1 is unique among all the hundreds of sacred books of the various religions of the world. With those words, we are confronted with the simple, implied request: do we *believe* what God says?

This first verse of the Bible refutes all of man's false philosophies about origins and the meaning of the world.

- It repudiates atheism because the universe was created by *God*.

- It repudiates pantheism because *God is transcendent* to all that He created.

- It repudiates polytheism because *only one God* created all things.

- It repudiates materialism because *matter had a beginning*.

- It repudiates dualism because *God was alone* when He created.

- It repudiates humanism because *God*, not man, *is the ultimate reality*.

- It repudiates evolutionism because God *created* all things.

The Creation Account Does Not Match Evolutionary Progression

Furthermore, the biblical record is not at all compatible with the story of evolution. Several foundational premises are in conflict with each other. Some hybrid theories of what could be called "crevolution"—devised by Christians—insist that the creation account in Scripture describes an order of development that is essentially the same as the order of evolutionary development. That is simply not so.

Those who propose such nonsense are either ignorant of what is recorded in Genesis, or they deliberately preach falsehood to make their particular brand of hybrid compromise fit the atheistic "story" of evolutionary science. Even a quick glance at the Genesis record manifests irresolvable conflicts.

The Biblical Record	Evolution's Order
Matter was created by God.	Matter has forever existed.
Earth was created before the sun and stars.	The sun and stars existed before earth.
The ocean was formed before land.	Land existed before the ocean.
There was light before the sun.	The sun was the earth's first light.
Land plants were earth's first life.	Marine organisms were earth's first life.
Plants were created before the sun.	The sun existed long before plants.
Fruit trees were created before fish.	Fish existed long before fruit trees.
Birds were created before insects.	Insects existed long before birds.
Birds were created before reptiles.	Reptiles existed before birds.
Man lived before there was rain.	Rain fell before man existed.
Man was created before the woman.	A female *Homo sapiens* was first.
Man was uniquely formed in perfection.	Man took ages to develop from apes.
The creation is finished.	Evolutionary "creation" is ongoing.

Perhaps one could say that the account in Genesis shows a "simple-to-complex" progression of creation, but the biblical progression is absolutely out of sequence with evolutionary theory. The specificity of the information in Genesis, in total agreement with the many other passages in the Bible that speak of the creation week, is so obviously different than the order of evolutionary development that one wonders why there is even an attempt to compare the two. The evolutionists will never accept these hybrid theories.

The Role of Death

One final thought. Evolution is dependent on death. Death, for the evolutionist, can only be a "good" process intended to weed out the "unfit" and make the "survival of the fittest" possible. Without the death of countless billions of life forms over eons of unrecorded time, evolution could not occur. For the evolutionist, therefore, death and time are absolute necessities—the key elements that make the process possible.

On the other hand, the biblical record introduces death as a judgment, a "curse" by the Creator on the fallen creation (Genesis 3:17-19). Death is an intrusion into that which God had pronounced "very good" when He evaluated His week of creative activity on the sixth day. Death is identified in the Bible as the "enemy" (1 Corinthians 15:26) that will be destroyed by the Creator in the "new heaven and new earth" (Revelation 21:1, 4). According to the biblical record, death did not enter the world until Adam, the steward and co-regent given responsibility for the care of the creation, dared to rebel against his Creator and was sentenced and banned from the garden in Eden (Romans 5:12).

These many and obvious conflicts between the historical record of creation in Scripture and the evolutionary story of origins ought to settle the issue for Christians, certainly for those who insist that they really believe that the Bible is God's holy Word. The Bible is clear, precise, and comprehensive in its presentation of the evidence for creation. That should be enough—even if "science" declares that the Bible is wrong.

Reason 2

Science Does Not Observe Evolution Happening Today

Anyone with a basic education (or even access to television) knows that science is based on observation and experimentation. Scientists in every discipline follow the rules of the famous "scientific method" when investigating phenomena and acquiring new knowledge.

Simply put, a hypothesis (i.e., an educated guess) is formed, based on observation or a prediction, then it is tested and the results are analyzed. If the test results repeatedly verify what was anticipated by the hypothesis, then the "scientific method" is said to have "proven" the theory.

Experimental Science

In the pure sciences (physics, chemistry, biology, etc.), the evidence must be observable and measurable, and the experiment itself must be repeatable. In the applied sciences (engineering, medicine, pharmacology, etc.), the testing is more rigorous, since unknown information may well result in the kind of failure that will do great damage. Many scientists would insist that to be satisfactorily proven, the hypothesis must be "falsifiable" as well. That standard—which, by the way, is demanded in courts of law whenever scientific evidence is used in a case—simply means that one must understand the processes and procedures used in the testing of the theory so well that the "wrong" answer must be also known. The scientist must understand the information so thoroughly that he would know what would *disprove* his theory. This level of rigor is applied by most experimental scientists today.

Adaptive or Directed Change Is Not Evolution

Although many experiments have attempted to duplicate some form of evolutionary change (e.g., from a lower form of life to a higher form, or from a mixture of chemicals to some kind of reproducing life form), no one has ever come close to "evolving" anything in the laboratory. Certain kinds of "change" can be replicated, such as mutations, which have often produced hideous results in various creatures. But the most brilliant scientists using the most expensive and advanced equipment cannot transform a "lower" form of life into a "higher" form.

And yet, evolutionary scientists and philosophers strongly believe this to be possible. They insist that since we can see *adaptive* (horizontal) change among living things (such as big dogs and little dogs), there must be *evolutionary* (vertical) change among living things over long periods of time (such as some common ancestor developing into both dogs and cats).

Nothing like *that* is observed in the present.

Scientists have, through selective breeding, made some pretty severe changes to the shapes and sizes of animals. For instance, there are over 450 breeds of dogs—everything from a tiny Chihuahua to the enormous Great Dane and Afghan Wolfhound. But they are still dogs. Never once has one of these dogs ever changed into a horse or a pig. The same can be said for cats. Although the Cat Fanciers' Association recognizes only 39 breeds of cats, all of the various sizes, shapes, and colors are still cats.

Change among kinds of creatures can "happen" or be made to happen, but those changes are always, *always* observed to remain within very specific and defined limits. Ever since humanity has been able to study these issues, there has never been a change from one kind of animal to another.

Evolutionary theory insists that somewhere back in the unobserved past, a common ancestor to both dogs and cats (possibly a small, meat-eating animal called *creodont*) began to "evolve" over time into the different kinds of animals that we now recognize as dogs and cats. However, there is no evidence for such changes—not in the present, certainly, and not in the fossil record. There are no "cogs" or "dats" anywhere! Finches, for example, may display variations in beak sizes in isolated population groups (as in Darwin's Galapagos Islands). However, finches do not become woodpeckers. Nor do fish become amphibians. There are no "fincheckers" and there are no "fishibians." Modern science observes absolutely no upward evolution taking place today—anywhere.

Natural Selection Is a Conservative Process

Natural selection is the process whereby natural environments tend to cull the least fit from some populations. Natural selection, as it has been observed, conserves. It preserves and protects a species; it does not innovate. Natural selection only "selects" from among what already exists. By itself, it does not add genetic information. Natural selection does indeed "weed out" the weaker and deformed creatures, but it has never been observed to "create" a new kind. Never!

Mutations to the DNA, on the other hand, do change the genetic information. Mutations disrupt the "code" and cause changes to the life-building process. Most mutations are "accidents" in the highly complex and vast information instructions of the genome. And most mutations are so small that their effect is virtually unremarkable. Those mutations, however, that impact the genetic information to the point that they make an observable change, are overwhelmingly negative; they are not beneficial. The unusual creatures that do reach live birth with these observable mutations either die before maturity, or are ignored by the rest of the population and do not reproduce. Thus, natural selection preserves or conserves the generic characteristics of that kind, eliminating the "mistakes" that happen.

No one has observed the evolutionary process of upward change taking place today. It does not happen. The false reasoning used by evolutionists is that "since there is evidence of small changes (horizontal), there must be big changes (vertical) over time." This may be logical *supposition*, but it is not *observation*—and it is not fact.

Reason 3

There Is No Evidence Evolution Took Place in the Past

Since it is impossible to conduct an experiment that either verifies or falsifies theories that take place over eons of time, one must turn to historical or forensic science for answers.

Historical or Forensic Science

Historical science observes clues in the present that may be applied to a possible cause in the past. For instance, archaeologists and paleontologists study origins just as detectives study a murder case. Both practice forensic (or historical) science, which uses the technical information and skills of the present to piece together the "remains" of a past event or sequence of events.

The archaeologist tries to "picture" what a given culture, city, or person may have looked like from the various remnants of civilization that are uncovered from that period of time. The paleontologist does essentially the same thing, but is looking at fossilized bones, trying to understand what a creature looked like, and when and how it lived, based on the information preserved in the earth's crust.

To develop forensic theories about the life forms of the ancient past, paleontologists turn to the fossil record. Almost all prehistorical evidence is contained in the fossil record. And almost all fossils are contained in various types of water-deposited rock (rare exceptions being those found in amber, peat, etc.). This sedimentary rock was distributed and laid down by water. And that water-deposited rock is all over the planet—even at the tops of mountains.

In order for evolutionary scientists to demonstrate that simple life forms have changed into more complex life forms over time, they must demonstrate it *historically* by producing examples of such changes, often referred to as "transitional" forms. If indeed the changes occurred slowly over "billions" of years through mutational accidents, then there ought to be many, many transitional remains available for scientists to uncover and observe in the fossil record.

And there ought to be an easily observed progressive order to the fossil record. That is, down at the deepest level of the water-deposited rock layers (supposedly the most ancient deposits), there should be very "simple" life forms like algae and other single-cell organisms. Further up in the layers (and supposedly nearer to our time), there should be more complex marine invertebrate creatures, with plenty of evidence of the transitional forms that changed from one-cell life to increasingly complex ocean life. Those creatures should have "evolved" into fish (and they should be found "higher" up in the water-deposited rock layers), and fish into amphibians, and amphibians into reptiles, etc.

The Evidence of the Fossil Record

That's what the evolutionary theory predicted would be found in the fossil record of our ancient past. However, the reality is far from what was expected.

Ninety-five percent of all fossils are marine invertebrates. These highly complex creatures (trilobites, starfish, coral, sponges, jellyfish, clams, ammonites, etc.) are found on the tops of mountains, in the middle of deserts, on all land masses on the earth—in *every* layer of the various "eras" of the proposed evolutionary time. The so-called geologic column is full of these marine invertebrates. These fossils are so abundant that the evolutionists themselves have named the era the "Cambrian Explosion." The organisms all appear fully formed, with absolutely no hint that they evolved from anything else. This layer of "first life" seems to "explode" in the fossil record, with no incontrovertible *observable* history prior to their existence.

That's a real problem for an evolutionary scientist. But it's exactly what would be expected by one who believes the information found in the Bible.

Of the remaining five percent of all fossils, 95 percent are plant fossils, typically part of coal beds and seams found everywhere on earth, including the well-known mountain ranges. These coal beds are even found in Antarctica. Ninety-five percent of what is left is comprised mostly of insect fossils (about .02 percent of the whole). And only about .01 percent of all fossils are the so-called "higher order" fossils. This provides very little evidence to work with, and many of these remains are merely pieces of fossilized bone—or are so jumbled together that it is almost impossible to tell which bone goes to which creature. Scientists have very little historical evidence to work with when trying to reconstruct the "later" life forms.

The animals that do exist as complete fossils (mostly marine creatures) are fully formed. The rare larger animals like the dinosaurs and extinct mammals are, in most cases, fragmented or crushed and broken so much that it is very difficult to tell what they really looked like. But in no case is there evidence for "transitional" forms—other than the fanciful stories invented by theorists and artists for museums and *National Geographic* specials.

Some fossilized creatures once thought to be extinct for "millions" of years are still in existence today, the famous Coelacanth fish being the best-known example. There are, in fact, a profusion of such living fossils found in exactly the same form as in the fossil record.[1] In addition, there are many life forms that are alive and prospering whose ancestors are found in the fossil record in essentially the same shape and size as we know them (e.g., the crocodile, the turtle, the bat, many fish, many insects). None of these has "transitioned" into anything else over the supposed millions of years of their existence, and there continues to be no fossil evidence (alive, extinct, or unique) that shows the slightest hint of them becoming another kind of creature.

Of course, speculation abounds about how they "could have" done this or that, or how the unusual features of some fossil "might have" developed into a leg or a wing or some other enormous structural change from what is observed on the fossil. But there is no evidence of such change. There is no *observed* transitional form. What certainly exists in huge quantities is *faith*—faith in a worldview of unobservable evolutionary development that excludes any supernatural intervention or direction of natural processes.

Evolutionary Faith

Faith in an evolutionary worldview, however, does not depend on evidence. The theory of evolution is a means to an end. The sole and stated purpose of a naturalistic or mechanistic cosmogony is to provide an atheistic explanation for the existence of all things. Repeatedly in the scientific literature, proponents of evolution insist that God—or any other supernatural force—cannot exist; materialism alone solves the needs of the soul.

---

1. Morris, H. M. 2000. The Profusion of Living Fossils. *Acts & Facts*. 29 (11).

Harvard professor Richard Lewontin, a geneticist, biologist, and social commentator, wrote an article published in *The New York Review* some years ago that explained why he and his peers were so committed to an atheistic and materialistic worldview:

> Our willingness to accept scientific claims that are against common sense is the key to an understanding of the real struggle between science and the supernatural. We take the side of science in spite of its failure to fulfill many of its extravagant promises of health and life, in spite of the tolerance of the scientific community for just-so stories, because we have a prior commitment to materialism.
>
> It is not that the methods and institutions of science somehow compel us to accept a material explanation of the phenomenal world, but, on the contrary, that we are forced by our a priori adherence to material causes to create an apparatus of investigation and a set of concepts that produce material explanations, no matter how counter-intuitive, no matter how mystifying to the uninitiated. Moreover that materialism is absolute for we cannot allow a Divine foot in the door.[2]

The story of evolution does not have the scientific evidence to support its assertions. What it does possess is an unyielding resolve to erase God's authority over creation.

---

2. Lewontin, R. C. 1997. Billions and Billions of Demons: Review of *The Demon-Haunted World: Science as a Candle in the Dark* by Carl Sagan. *The New York Review of Books.* 44 (1): 31.

REASON 4

GOD'S CHARACTER ABSOLUTELY FORBIDS EVOLUTIONARY METHODS

Everything God has created reveals His eternal power and triune nature in such a way that man has no excuse for not recognizing Him as Creator.

> For the invisible things of him from the creation of the world are clearly seen, being understood by the things that are made, even his eternal power and Godhead; so that they are without excuse. (Romans 1:20)

Our universe is so vast that man has so far been unable to observe even the boundaries of space. The reservoirs of power that can be observed are so huge that there is no way of understanding "how" or "why" they came into being. Educated guesses abound (some of them pretty complex and fanciful—like the Big Bang), but all one can really *know* is that the power seems both "eternal" and "infinite."

Time itself is a great mystery. Its existence is unquestioned, and careful attention is given to its passing. Man uses time and functions within it, but no one really understands what time is, how it came to be, or how to control it. What can be understood is that everything that exists, exists *in* space and *through* time. Even the mass-energy (matter) seen and experienced every day consists of various forms of energy in motion during time that produce specific phenomena (e.g., molecules, trees, planets, people, etc.) in which "we live, and move, and have our being" (Acts 17:28).

A Universe of Space, Matter, and Time

The universe is both *uni* (one) and *verse* (different). And while something of the three different manifestations of reality (space, matter, time) can be understood, they cannot be separated from the "unit."

Space is invisible and "empty," but it is obviously not "nothing." No one knows just what it is. Matter is similarly indefinable. Atoms can be split into small pieces, but not even the most gifted scientist can "make" an atom. In fact, one of the most universal laws of man's reality is that "matter can neither be created nor destroyed." The universe could not have created itself.

Man's understanding about the way the universe functions is both simple and profound. Space is the omnipresent background and source of all reality. Everything that exists both resides in space and occupies space. Only when mass-energy (matter) moving in and through time produces a phenomenon (an event) does space become evident, allowing man to observe the various things that exist in space (e.g., galaxies, stars, planets, trees, people). Space can be "seen" only when matter is present.

But to experience anything, time is essential. Matter itself is an ongoing manifestation of complex energies functioning in a specific manner *during* time. A "lifetime" is just that: life functioning in and through time. For instance, if I wish to "experience" my wife (give her a hug or a good-morning kiss), I must use time to cross the space to where her particular form of mass-energy exists, and reduce the space that separates us so that we can actually make contact with each other.

The Signature of God in the Heavens

Why labor through all of this difficult explanation about space and matter and time? What bearing does this have on the character of God and the impossibility of evolutionary methods? Just this: the Bible clearly states that the created things provide a "clearly seen" illustration of the power and divine nature of the Creator. The universe becomes the "speech" and "language" of God that reveal Him to all humanity (Psalm 19:1-4). Put in a chart form, it would look something like this:

The TRI-UNE God		
Manifested by and analogous to His creation		
Father = SPACE	Son = MATTER	Spirit = TIME
Invisible	Visible	Sensed & Felt
Omnipresent	Tangible	Understood
Source	Present Reality	Future
God Framed	God Manifested	God Experienced
Authority	Declaration	Appropriation
Deuteronomy 6:4		

God's creation is a "picture" of what He is like. God the Father is the invisible, omnipresent background and source of all things. He is transcendent beyond the creation, yet He is ever-present and everywhere present—just like the Bible describes in Psalm 139.

> Whither shall I go from thy spirit? or whither shall I flee from thy presence? If I ascend up into heaven, thou art there: if I make my bed in hell, behold, thou art there. (Psalm 139:7-8)

But He is also quite visible in the person of the only begotten Son of God, the Lord Jesus Christ. There are a number of Bible passages that teach this marvelous truth. Here are three of the more obvious sections.

> In the beginning was the Word, and the Word was with God, and the Word was God....And the Word was made flesh, and dwelt among us, (and we beheld his glory, the glory as of the only begotten of the Father,) full of grace and truth. (John 1:1, 14)

> Jesus saith unto him, Have I been so long time with you, and yet hast thou not known me, Philip? he that hath seen me hath seen the Father. (John 14:9)

> For in [Christ] dwelleth all the fulness of the Godhead bodily. (Colossians 2:9)

Just like space is made visible and understandable by matter, so God the Son, the Messiah, Jesus of Nazareth, makes God the Father visible and understandable by His presence on earth. And just like space and matter are "one" in the sense that they are inseparable and coterminous at all times, so God the Father and God the Son are "one" (John 10:30).

And indeed, just as time is the vital element through which mankind can "experience" everything that can be known in his small part of the universe, so God the Holy Spirit is the person of the triune Godhead through whom man is enabled to "experience" both the Father and the Son. Again, there are many Bible passages that tell of the Holy Spirit's role in salvation, spiritual guidance, and growing awareness of the person and work of Christ. Here are a few of the more obvious texts.

> If I go not away, the Comforter will not come unto you....
> And when he is come, he will reprove the world of sin, and

of righteousness, and of judgment. (John 16:7-8)

God hath from the beginning chosen you to salvation through sanctification of the Spirit and belief of the truth. (2 Thessalonians 2:13)

That which is born of the Spirit is spirit. Marvel not that I said unto thee, Ye must be born again…so is every one that is born of the Spirit. (John 3:6-8)

Howbeit when he, the Spirit of truth, is come, he will guide you into all truth. (John 16:13)

The Godhead (Romans 1:20; Colossians 2:9) is the triune Deity who created the universe. That universe is the only accurate picture of His divine nature (2 Peter 1:4), having been created by God to provide a totally accessible foundation by which one can *know* that the Creator does exist (Romans 1:19-21). That universally available knowledge enables mankind to "believe that he is, and that he is a rewarder of them that diligently seek him" (Hebrews 11:6).

The one ongoing "creation" act that God continues to perform is the new birth of those who are "created in righteousness and true holiness" (Ephesians 4:24). Men and women are born into this world spiritually "dead in trespasses and sins" (Ephesians 2:1) and must be "passed from death unto life" (John 5:24). That change produces a new man (Colossians 3:10) that is "made free from sin" (Romans 6:18) so that everyone can be "partakers of the divine nature" (2 Peter 1:4), where "old things are passed away" and "all things are become new" (2 Corinthians 5:17).

The Holiness of God

The preeminent attribute of God is holiness. This unique nature both drives and limits God's revelation of Himself to His creation.

There is none holy as the LORD: for there is none beside thee. (1 Samuel 2:2; see also Exodus 15:11 and Isaiah 6:3)

This holiness requires truth. God cannot lie (Titus 1:2), and whenever God reveals anything, He must reveal the truth about Himself and His nature.

Wherein God, willing more abundantly to shew unto the heirs of promise the immutability of his counsel, confirmed

it by an oath: That by two immutable things, in which
it was impossible for God to lie, we might have a strong
consolation. (Hebrews 6:17-18; see also Psalm 89:33 and
Amos 4:2)

That biblical axiom is true whether applied to scientific research, educational philosophy, theological speculations, or heretical doctrine.

For what if some did not believe? shall their unbelief make
the faith of God without effect? God forbid: yea, let God
be true, but every man a liar. (Romans 3:3-4; see also John
14:6, Titus 1:1-3, and 1 John 5:20)

The incarnate Creator God must reveal truth, and that truth cannot
be an untruth. When God speaks, He must speak the truth; when God
acts, He must do the truth.

These things saith he that is holy, he that is true, he that hath
the key of David, he that openeth, and no man shutteth;
and shutteth, and no man openeth....These things saith the
Amen, the faithful and true witness, the beginning of the
creation of God. (Revelation 3:7, 14; see also John 8:31-32
and 2 Corinthians 1:18-20)

God's holiness demands that the creation not distort anything about
Him or about the creation itself. God could not create a lie. He could not
make anything that would inexorably lead to a wrong conclusion. God
could not create processes that would counter His own nature or that
would lead man to conclude something untrue about God.

Because of these sacred truths, the age-long processes required by
evolutionary naturalism are absolutely incompatible with the demands
of a holy Creator. The words of the biblical text do not use the same
order, the same language, or imply the same concepts. Since God is truly
holy, a very difficult and complex deconstruction and interpretation of
the text is necessary to allow for a combination or hybridization of these
two very different ideas. God's holiness required Him to create a perfect
garden, for instance, fully formed and beautiful at the moment of its first
creation.

It is because of man—once perfect, created last—that the world fell
to ruin.

The Omniscience of God

Today, the most easily observable attribute of God is His omniscience. The unlimited power of God (His omnipotence) is displayed in the apparently infinite universe containing the immeasurable energy resources in the uncounted galaxies of space. Certainly they speak of God's eternal power. But in the last few decades, humanity has become more aware of the infinitely complex nature of this universe. From the vast majesty of the stellar host to the minute beauty of microscopic living organisms, the incredible design and order of the world is becoming more and more evident.

The Universe Is an Infinite Reservoir of Information

Within the past decade, the vast information of the genome has stunned scientists. Not only are there "instructions" written for biological development of the specific life form, but there are languages within languages, repair codes, timing signals, duplication mechanisms—an entire "library" of information that is unique for each of the millions of reproducing living systems on earth. The old academic cliché "the more I know the more I know I don't know" has never been more true than it is today.

There is no such thing as a "simple" cell. If it is alive, it is *not* simple.

So where did the information come from? Certainly not from inanimate matter. Chemicals and amino acids and proteins are not information-generating systems. They may be part of the "letters" in the "words" of the instructions, but they do not *produce* the information. There is order and functioning precision at every level of the universe. How did such order and precision get there? Certainly not from an "explosion" and a random drift of interacting molecules. Randomness (chaos) never produces order and precision. The information so readily and easily observable in the universe fairly screams for a Designer.

The only reason not to believe in an omniscient Creator is that one *refuses* to believe.

The Bible Emphasizes God's Omniscience

Written throughout the text of God's Word are many sections that tell about the infinite mind of the Creator. His purposes and means are perfect and guided by wisdom and design, not allowed to drift randomly in confusion as an "evolutionary" God would be required to do. God's decisions do not change or falter, but are the assured perfection of holy goodness and absolute knowledge. Everything from the beginning of time has been determined "according to the good pleasure of his will" (Ephesians 1:5). Here are a few of the many Scriptures that speak of God's omniscience.

> I am God, and there is none else; I am God, and there is none like me, declaring the end from the beginning, and from ancient times the things that are not yet done, saying, My counsel shall stand, and I will do all my pleasure. (Isaiah 46:9-10)

> Known unto God are all his works from the beginning of the world. (Acts 15:18)

> …to the acknowledgement of the mystery of God, and of the Father, and of Christ; in whom are hid all the treasures of wisdom and knowledge. (Colossians 2:2-3)

Human language may not be sufficient to completely convey the entire concept of omniscience, but several key elements can be summarized this way:

- God is not unaware of anything.
- God cannot be progressively aware.
- God's knowledge is immediate.
- God is free from imperfection.
- God knows all there is to know.

God Keeps Some "Secrets"

Some things in God's plan for the universe, some of the future plans He has for man, are kept secret until the planned events become a reality. Some reasons and processes are far too complex for fallen man to comprehend. Much of the future would be terrifying to contemplate if the details were known in advance. It is far better for man to trust the all-knowing, loving, and patient Creator to reveal what he needs to know.

> The secret things belong unto the LORD our God: but those things which are revealed belong unto us and to our children for ever. (Deuteronomy 29:29; see also 1 Corinthians 13:12

and 2 Peter 1:3)

God, the omniscient One, *must* reveal complete information—or He *must* withhold information (the "secret things"). Any partial revelation, when presented as though it is all of the information, would be a lie. The so-called "half truth" is nothing but a sanitized term for a lie. God cannot lie, and therefore He cannot say or do anything that would be either partially true or imperfectly functioning. God can and sometimes does make statements that reveal large truths without giving specific details, such as, "My kingdom is not of this world" (John 18:36). But God would never speak or do anything that would mislead man.

God Is Never Random or Confused

There is no hint of "randomness" in God. God is never surprised so that He must react to unforeseen circumstances. Neither is God forced to change His mind about His reasons or His plans. He does not alter His plans for eternity, nor does He get confused about His design, His pleasure, or His purpose: "Whatsoever the LORD pleased, that did he in heaven, and in earth, in the seas, and all deep places" (Psalm 135:6). God's purposes are ordered and flow from His omniscience. His decisions are unchangeable and without confusion. His specific will and pleasure are always implemented.

> My counsel shall stand, and I will do all my pleasure....yea, I have spoken it, I will also bring it to pass; I have purposed it, I will also do it. (Isaiah 46:10-11; see also Psalm 33:11, 1 Corinthians 14:33, Ephesians 1:9-11, and Hebrews 6:17-19)

God's omniscience demands that God create only the absolute best, whether at the scale of the universe or the scale of the molecule. He could not, and would not, experiment. Since God knows what is best, He therefore must do that best. An omniscient God could not and would not produce an inferior product. He must create, shape, and make only that which is good. It is no accident or verbal hyperbole that the text of Genesis chapter one repeats the statement "and God saw that it was good." Neither is it merely poetic parallelism for the record to note that at the end of the sixth and final day of God's creating work, the text reads: "And God saw everything that he had made, and, behold, it was very good" (Genesis 1:31).

So-called *theistic evolution* (as well as the various other "Christian" attempts to hybridize the words of Scripture with the theories of naturalistic evolution) requires both experimentation with "creation" and the creation of inferior forms. In evolution, there is no permanent good. Evolutionary naturalism requires the use of processes and the sanction of activities that are contradictory to God's nature.

Back in the early 1990s there was a "revival" of theistic evolution, which received a good bit of favorable press through the Evangelical Theological Society and the American Scientific Affiliation—organizations that insisted that they support biblical inspiration, while seeing no difficulties in accepting evolutionary mechanisms as God's method of "creation." Professor David Hull wrote an article in the widely-read *Nature* magazine that made it very clear that even secular scientists recognize that the biblical account of creation and evolution are incompatible.

> The evolutionary process is rife with happenstance, contingency, incredible waste, death, pain and horror.... [Theistic evolution's God] is not a loving God who cares about His productions. [He] is careless, wasteful, indifferent, almost diabolical. He is certainly not the sort of God to whom anyone would be inclined to pray.[3]

Apparently, godless scholars are more aware of the impossibility of mixing the two belief systems than are those Christians who insist that there is no problem. Although significant time has elapsed since Dr. Hull wrote his critique of theistic evolution, the increase in the acceptance of the hybrid theories has only been eclipsed by the apathy of Christians who see no "importance" in the doctrine of creation.

---

3. Hull, D. L. 1991. The God of the Galapagos. *Nature*. 352 (6335): 486.

GOD'S PURPOSE FOR CREATION EXCLUDES EVOLUTION

The direct will of God was expressed through His act of creating:

> Thou art worthy, O Lord, to receive glory and honour and power: for thou hast created all things, and for thy pleasure they are and were created. (Revelation 4:11)

> For by him were all things created, that are in heaven, and that are in earth, visible and invisible...all things were created by him, and for him: And he is before all things, and by him all things consist. (Colossians 1:16-17)

> For of him, and through him, and to him, are all things: to whom be glory for ever. Amen. (Romans 11:36)

Once again, given what the Scriptures reveal about the nature of God, that the purpose of creating the universe was to *please* God and to *honor* God, it absolutely eliminates any possibility that the God of the Bible would have used any form of naturalistic evolution to "create" that which would forever speak of His person and work. If the words of Scripture are true words, if they are God's words, then there can be no "evolution" in God's work.

Creating Eliminated Any Excuse to Deny God's Existence

> For the invisible things of him from the creation of the world are clearly seen, being understood by the things that are made, even his eternal power and Godhead; so that they are without excuse. (Romans 1:20)

> The heavens declare the glory of God; and the firmament sheweth his handywork. Day unto day uttereth speech, and night unto night sheweth knowledge. There is no speech nor language, where their voice is not heard. (Psalm 19:1-3)

For some reason, many Christians seem to think that God is somehow unfair to those nations and people who haven't heard the gospel. In one way or another, subtle doubt about God's "favoritism" or "arbitrary" salvation methods creep into the personal theology of many, who try desperately to devise ways in which God gives a second chance or has a more "tolerant" judgment for those who don't have the chance to "accept Jesus as their personal Savior."

The Bible is clear. God has done everything necessary for all men to know that He exists. He has and He will "draw all men" to Christ (John 12:32). God will reveal Himself to all who seek for Him with "all [their] heart" (Jeremiah 29:13). Conversely, God will reject all those who change "the glory of the uncorruptible God into an image made like to corruptible man, and to birds, and fourfooted beasts, and creeping things" (Romans 1:23) and will deliver men to a "reprobate mind" who change "the truth of God into a lie, and worshipped and served the creature more than the Creator" (Romans 1:28, 25).

Creating Gave a Foundation to the Everlasting Gospel

> And I saw another angel fly in the midst of heaven, having the everlasting gospel to preach unto them that dwell on the earth…saying with a loud voice, Fear God, and give glory to him; for the hour of his judgment is come: and worship him that made heaven, and earth, and the sea, and the fountains of waters. (Revelation 14:6-7)

The gospel of Jesus Christ entails the full threefold work of Christ as the Creator, and the One who presently conserves all things, and who finally will consummate all things unto Himself (Colossians 1:16-17). If the creation message is neglected, there is no foundation for or evidence of the omnipotent ability of God to save. If the work of Christ on the cross of Calvary is neglected, then there is no reconciliation of God's holiness toward sinners. If the promise of a sinless, completely righteous, deathless future in a new heaven and new earth is neglected, then there is no hope. The "everlasting gospel" sits solidly on the foundation of the creation reality.

Creating Gave Authority to the Message of Jesus Christ

> For by him were all things created, that are in heaven, and that are in earth, visible and invisible…all things were created by him, and for him: and he is before all things, and by him all things consist. And he is the head of the body, the church: who is the beginning, the firstborn from

the dead; that in all things he might have the preeminence. (Colossians 1:16-18)

Jesus once said to His struggling disciples, "The words that I speak unto you I speak not of myself: but the Father that dwelleth in me, he doeth the works. Believe me that I am in the Father, and the Father in me: or else believe me for the very works' sake" (John 14:10-11). He said essentially the same thing to the unbelieving religious leaders: "Then came the Jews round about him, and said unto him, How long dost thou make us to doubt? If thou be the Christ, tell us plainly. Jesus answered them, I told you, and ye believed not: the works that I do in my Father's name, they bear witness of me" (John 10:24-25).

John's gospel is built around seven great miracles of creation. These were miracles that required the creation of new matter (water into wine); new functioning organs (the man born blind); new bone, muscles, nerves, etc. (the man with the withered arm). Again and again, Jesus demonstrated His *creation* power before the masses. It is of interest that "the common people heard him gladly" (Mark 12:37), but the religious leaders plotted to kill Him.

Creating Displayed the Power of Jesus Christ

In the beginning was the Word, and the Word was with God, and the Word was God. The same was in the beginning with God. All things were made by him; and without him was not any thing made that was made. In him was life; and the life was the light of men....But as many as received him, to them gave he power to become the sons of God, even to them that believe on his name....And the Word was made flesh, and dwelt among us, (and we beheld his glory, the glory as of the only begotten of the Father,) full of grace and truth. (John 1:1-4, 12, 14)

Although this is similar to the authority issue, the emphasis in John's opening statement about "the Word" is that He was God from eternity past, equal in every respect as the Son of God within the Trinity, yet He "was made flesh" and entered the world that He had created in order to redeem those whom He had created. That truth gives the substitutionary work of Jesus Christ both its legitimacy as the fully human substitute for humanity, and its infinite power as the full Deity and Creator to satisfy the judgment of a Holy God for the "sins of the whole world" (1 John 2:2).

Creating Is How God Gives New Life

> For by grace are ye saved through faith; and that not of yourselves: it is the gift of God: Not of works, lest any man should boast. For we are his workmanship, created in Christ Jesus unto good works, which God hath before ordained that we should walk in them. (Ephesians 2:8-10)

Even though God rested from His *creation* of the space-matter-time universe on the seventh day, He continues *creating* the "new man" as men and women and children of all ages come to Him as Redeemer and Savior.

For this, as well as for all the other great works of the Lord Jesus Christ, mankind should be forever grateful. You and I should be grateful. He is now sitting in the throne room of heaven mediating and serving as High Priest and Advocate for us; therefore, we should constantly praise Him. Since He is the One who will one day (perhaps soon) reign as King of kings and Lord of lords, we should expectantly pray for His kingdom to "come" and for His will to be "done in earth, as it is in heaven" (Matthew 6:10).

Even so, Lord Jesus, come quickly.

APPENDIX A

THE FOUNDATIONAL IMPORTANCE OF BIBLICAL CREATIONISM

Biblical creationism is foundational to all Christian doctrine. Christ was Creator before He became Redeemer (Colossians 1:16, John 1:3, Hebrews 1:3). Unless, therefore, the presentation of the person and work of Christ is based on His role as Creator, what is being taught is actually "another Jesus." Paul strongly warns against such false teaching and perversions of the gospel of Christ in 2 Corinthians 11:4 and Galatians 1:7-8.

The first object of a living faith and a saving faith (Hebrews 10:38-39) is a solid belief in special creation: "Through faith we understand that the worlds were framed by the word of God, so that things which are seen were not made of things which do appear" (Hebrews 11:3). This negates theistic evolution, which assumes that everything in the present was created from other things in the past. It therefore demands a meaningful faith built on special creation.

Biblical creationism is the foundation of true evangelism. John's gospel is built on the first through third verses of his first chapter: "In the beginning was the Word." This same phrase begins the first book of the Bible and ties it to the importance of knowing the creating work of Christ. When Christians confess that "Jesus is the Christ, the Son of God" so that they "might have life through his name," they are confessing to a belief in every aspect of Christ's nature and role, including His role as Creator (John 20:31).

True missions also begin with biblical creationism. When the polytheistic evolutionists of Lystra were given the gospel, they were reprimanded with the following words: "Ye should turn from these vanities unto the living God, which made heaven, and earth, and the sea, and all things that are therein" (Acts 14:15). And to the atheistic evolutionist Epicureans and the pantheistic evolutionist Stoics in Athens was written, "God that made the world and all things therein...is Lord of heaven and earth" (Acts 17:24). When Paul delivered the gospel to people who already believed in the Scriptures, including creation, he always began at Jesus and gave the gospel of the cross and resurrection. But to those who did not believe, he began with the creation truth.

Biblical creationism is the foundation of true Bible teaching. When Christ spoke on the road to Emmaus, "beginning at Moses and all the prophets, he expounded unto them in all the scriptures the things concerning himself" (Luke 24:27). Christ revealed Himself to His walking companions beginning with the first things: His creative work recorded in the words of Moses.

Paul's goal in his preaching to the churches was to show them the true "fellowship of the mystery, which from the beginning of the world hath been hid in God, who created all things by Jesus Christ: to the intent that now unto the principalities and powers in heavenly places might be known by the church the manifold wisdom of God" (Ephesians 3:9-10). God's creating work gives the church a common theme in its worship and a fellowship as children of their Creator.

Recognizing God as first above all Creator and head of the church is the start of a hierarchy that He models. Christ details that hierarchy with concern to the household and family relationships in Matthew.

> And he answered and said unto them, Have ye not read, that he which made them at the beginning made them male and female, and said, For this cause shall a man leave father and mother, and shall cleave to his wife: and they twain shall be one flesh? Wherefore they are no more twain, but one flesh. What therefore God hath joined together, let not man put asunder. (Matthew 19:4-6)

Christ is the head of the church, being the firstborn of all creation, just as man is head over his wife, having been created before her.

Biblical creationism also provides a model for all human vocations. In Genesis 1:28, God gave the Dominion Mandate: "Be fruitful and multiply, and replenish the earth, and subdue it: and have dominion over the fish of the sea, and over the fowl of the air, and over every living thing that moveth upon the earth." This primeval command implies all honorable human occupations.

- Science for the purpose of understanding the earth;
- Technology for the purpose of developing it;
- Commerce to utilize it;
- Education to transmit the knowledge of it;

- Humanities for the purpose of glorifying it.

Every occupation may be used in some way to glorify God and recognize man's responsibility to God's creation by obeying this first command of dominion over the earth. Beyond occupational services to God's creation, man has his own specific purpose. Although the image of God in man has been marred by sin, when he is created again by the new birth, he can then begin to live the kind of life for which God created man in the beginning. The new creature may be daily renewed to be more like his Father and closer to the holiness that he was intended to know (2 Corinthians 5:17; Colossians 3:20; Ephesians 4:24).

Once a biblical worldview has been adopted, including a proper understanding of creation and redemption, the Christian believer will rightly relate to other Christians, society around him, and the Creator Redeemer Himself who has reconciled all things to God. In order for the true gospel to be preached, the full scope of God's work must be told, for it is only the true gospel, wholly and uncompromising, that is the power of God unto salvation (Romans 1:16). This gospel encompasses the threefold work of Christ: creation, conservation, and consummation. If the gospel story neglects the creation of the past, there is no foundation, standard, or ability. If it neglects the cross, there is no authority, justness, or power. And if it neglects the coming kingdom, there is no hope or joy or victory.

The church has been working hard and effectually on the central aspect of the gospel, but it is time to reaffirm its commitment to preach the whole "counsel of God" (Acts 20:27) and teach the foundation and consummation of God's wondrous work as well.

Adapted from Morris, H. M. 2000. *Biblical Creationism*. Green Forest, AR: Master Books, 228-232.

Appendix B

Reclaiming the Full Gospel Message

Christians possess a divine privilege that the world cannot have: they have been given the mind of Christ (1 Corinthians 2:16) and are empowered by the Holy Sprit to know the truth (1 John 2:20). But the church has deferred much of this gift to the popular scientific ideas of today, abandoning its divine right to the truth.

It has become popular to believe that winning souls is more important than adhering to the clear biblical truth—that if certain biblical doctrines conflict with the conclusions of secular science, they can be ignored or cast aside in order to "by all means save some" (1 Corinthians 9:22). However, this is the very reason why so many churches are still doctrinally and morally weak. Many, many people are thirsting for something stronger than ambiguous stories and unanswered questions on the origins of life, and they seek confirmation of the holy nature of a God who is often portrayed as cruel and untrustworthy.

How can the church impact the world for Christ if so many professing Christians mistrust their God and the revelation He gave to them? Why accommodate the secular and often blatantly atheistic world, when the biblical worldview answers the many questions that the world cannot? The Bible offers the power of the true gospel, and despite the protestations of a relativistic culture, people are hungry for the truth.

The Central Gospel Message

Almost every person who has gone to a Christian church knows that Christ commanded His disciples to reach the whole world with the proclamation of the gospel message. The New Testament Greek word most often translated "gospel" is *euaggelion* (in English, "evangelion"). The verb form is *euaggelizo*, from which our English word "evangelize" is derived. The basic meaning of those two Greek words simply means a "good message." The English word "gospel" is shortened from the Saxon phrase "God Spell," meaning God's news.

It is interesting to note that "gospel" appears precisely 101 times in the New Testament. Centrally positioned right in the middle of these references—fifty before and fifty after—is 1 Corinthians 15:1-4.

> Moreover, brethren, I declare unto you the gospel which I preached unto you, which also ye have received, and wherein ye stand; By which also ye are saved, if ye keep in memory what I preached unto you, unless ye have believed in vain. For I delivered unto you first of all that which I also received, how that Christ died for our sins according to the scriptures; and that he was buried, and that he rose again the third day according to the scriptures.

This passage is the defining passage for the gospel. The focus is the death, physical burial, and bodily resurrection of Christ. This message is to be received and believed by faith, once and for all. It is the means by which men are saved, continually and forever. These are *the* facts—the unyielding truth—upon which men may firmly stand. They are emphatically defined, understood by means of, and declared "according to the scriptures." The gospel is not to be adapted to fit the context of one's environment or personal preference: It is to be proclaimed singularly, precisely, and persistently, as an absolute truth that God has revealed.

Apart from the work of Jesus Christ on the cross, there is no forgiveness.

The Hope of the Gospel

Most certainly the forgiveness of our sins is "good news." Our sins are cast behind the "back" of God (Isaiah 38:17). They have been removed from us "as far as the east is from the west" (Psalm 103:12), and from the human perspective those sins have been cast "into the depths of the sea" (Micah 7:19). But as marvelously wonderful as that knowledge may be, there is more!

The first reference concerning the gospel is recorded in Matthew 4:23. Christ came "preaching the gospel of the kingdom." In the very beginning of His ministry, Jesus announced (preached) the good news that He was there to fulfill (to consummate) the promises made to the patriarchs for those who were or would become "His people." One day, Jesus Christ will be acknowledged by all creation to be the "king of kings and lord of lords" (Revelation 17:14). For those who have received His grace-gift of salvation (John 1:12), the recognition before the great throne in the courts of heaven will be a joy "unspeakable and full of glory" (1 Peter 1:8). For those who have rejected His love and spurned the witness of the Holy Spirit, the awful realization of their eternal damnation will come in a "whirlwind" of fear and destruction (Proverbs 1:27).

The "good news" part of the message of the gospel is summarized in the last two chapters of Revelation. The new Jerusalem, the capital city of King Jesus, is described in these glorious passages, and a formal declaration is given by God to the redeemed:

> And I heard a great voice out of heaven saying, Behold, the tabernacle of God is with men, and he will dwell with them, and they shall be his people, and God himself shall be with them, and be their God. And God shall wipe away all tears from their eyes; and there shall be no more death, neither sorrow, nor crying, neither shall there be any more pain: for the former things are passed away. (Revelation 21:3-4)

An absolutely vital part of the gospel is the stunning news that our salvation will consummate in a permanent and eternal "new heavens and a new earth, wherein dwelleth righteousness" (2 Peter 3:13). This future hope of a righteous life for eternity with the Creator-God even sustained the Lord Jesus as He faced the horrible and ignominious death by crucifixion: "Who for the joy that was set before him endured the cross, despising the shame" (Hebrews 12:2). Paul the Apostle made the comment, "If in this life only we have hope in Christ, we are of all men most miserable" (1 Corinthians 15:19).

Apart from the promise of a future eternal righteous life, there is no hope.

The Authority for the Gospel Message

And yet there is more. Indeed, there *must* be more! Where does the authority to grant forgiveness come from? Where does the power to rebuild a universe in perfection come from? How can sinful men be made sinless? Where? How? What can we "see" that will assure us that the promises of forgiveness and an eternal destiny of righteousness will be "real"?

Yes, Jesus Christ rose from the grave, having conquered death, and gave "assurance unto all men" (Acts 17:31). That, too, is part of the gospel (Romans 10:9). But where did that power come from? How can we find "faith" in that which is so supernatural that our natural minds see only "foolishness" (1 Corinthians 2:14)?

God did not leave the answers to that problem out of His "good news." Part and parcel to the gospel is the unshakable foundation and omnipotent display of the creation of the universe.

The very last verse in the Bible to cite the gospel extends the scope of the "good message" to the "everlasting gospel." This section in Revelation 14 tells of a mighty angel who is commissioned to fly throughout the entire atmosphere of the earth:

> ...having the everlasting gospel to preach unto them that dwell on the earth, and to every nation, and kindred, and tongue, and people, saying with a loud voice, Fear God, and give glory to him; for the hour of his judgment is come: and worship him that made heaven, and earth, and the sea, and the fountains of waters. (Revelation 14:6-7)

Here the emphasis is on the creation—the origin of the "good message." The same Jesus who hung on the cross of Calvary as the full substitute for the sins of the whole world is the same One who *created* the whole world. The same One who cried out in the most incomprehensible statement of grace and mercy ever uttered, "Father, forgive them; for they know not what they do" (Luke 23:34), is the same One who simply commanded: "Let there be light: and there was light" (Genesis 1:3).

> For by him were all things created, that are in heaven, and that are in earth, visible and invisible, whether they be thrones, or dominions, or principalities, or powers: all things were created by him, and for him: And he is before all things, and by him all things consist. And he is the head of the body, the church: who is the beginning, the firstborn from the dead; that in all things he might have the preeminence. For it pleased the Father that in him should all fullness dwell; And, having made peace through the blood of his cross, by him to reconcile all things unto himself; by him, I say, whether they be things in earth, or things in heaven. (Colossians 1:16-20)

The Full Gospel

The gospel message entails the full scope of the work of Jesus Christ, involving the whole sweep of His redemptive purpose in history. Everything from the beginning of creation to the triumphal day when every living creature, at last, will confess the truth of Christ's lordship (Philippians 2:11) is part of God's great redemptive plan. The gospel does not finish with a mere salvation from death, just as it does not begin with Christ's death on the cross. It begins with His work of creation.

It is Christ who first created the heavens and earth, and having created them, ended His creative work (Colossians 1:16). All things continue to exist, conserved as mass and energy (v. 17), but it is by His will alone, for His purposes, and for His sake that creation continues its existence. Finally, these verses speak of the beautiful reconciliation made by Christ's death, not only with man, but with the creation itself (v. 20). Through Christ's blood, earth and heaven may be restored to harmony. No longer an enemy of God, this once alienated world may be brought again into a universal concord conformed to the government of its Creator.

Hebrews 1:2-3 reiterates that God, through Christ, created the worlds, and that it is Christ who will be the heir of all things—the nations and the earth—as reigning Lord (Psalm 2:8), "for of him, and through him, and to him, are all things: to whom be glory for ever. Amen" (Romans 11:36). The gospel of the Lord Jesus Christ encompasses a threefold work: creation, conservation, and consummation. Christ was present before time began, He continues His work of upholding His creation, and one day He will be finally recognized as King and Lord of all.

In the past, present, and future, God's love and glory are evident in His great work of creation, and every part of His plan must be addressed in the gospel if it is to be proclaimed with confidence in its everlasting truth. If the act of creation is neglected in the presentation of the gospel, then the very foundation of God's plan is lost and the authority He has over life and all things is forgotten. If the cross is neglected, then Christ has no authority over death, and no power of salvation or reconciliation to God.

To neglect the kingdom is to abandon any hope or present joy.

For More Information

Sign up for ICR's FREE publications!

Our monthly *Acts & Facts* magazine offers fascinating articles and current information on creation, evolution, and more. Our quarterly *Days of Praise* booklet provides daily devotionals—real biblical "meat"—to strengthen and encourage the Christian witness.

To subscribe, call 800.337.0375 or mail your address information to the address below. Or sign up online at www.icr.org.

Visit ICR online

ICR.org offers a wealth of resources and information on scientific creationism and biblical worldview issues.

✓ Read our daily news postings on today's hottest science topics

✓ Explore the Evidence for Creation

✓ Investigate our graduate and professional education programs

✓ Dive into our archive of 40 years of scientific articles

✓ Listen to current and past radio programs

✓ Order creation science materials online

✓ And more!

For a list of ICR resources, visit icr.org/store

Institute for Creation Research

P. O. Box 59029
Dallas, TX 75229
800.337.0375
www.icr.org